★American Girl®

Inspiring Stories From the Past

INSIGHT
KIDS

SAN RAFAEL · LOS ANGELES · LO[

T0019412

MEET KAYA

NAME: Kaya

NICKNAMES: Magpie

HOME: Salmon River Country
(Present-day Idaho)

HAIR: Black   EYES: Brown

DREAMS OF: Becoming a courageous
leader of the Nez Perce tribe

YEAR: 1764

Kaya races her horse, Steps High, against Fox Tail and Raven.
Steps High runs like the wind and almost bucks Kaya off her back!

Kaya and her sister Speaking Rain are taken by raiders.
They are forced to work in the raiders' camp until Kaya makes her escape.

Kaya befriends a captive named Two Hawks, and they escape together.
They journey through the dangerous forest, and Kaya is reunited with her tribe.

KAYA'S WORLD WORD SEARCH

Find and circle the words listed below by searching up, down, forward, backward, and diagonally.

```
F  W  H  Q  Y  T  D  F  E  Y
T  R  I  V  E  R  R  I  H  Y
L  U  K  M  L  M  P  V  K  J
O  I  D  X  L  G  U  M  A  O
K  L  J  U  A  I  R  T  Y  N
T  A  N  M  V  F  Y  Y  A  N
S  R  E  D  I  A  R  L  E  O
N  Q  H  X  L  B  D  Z  Q  T
V  O  W  O  L  U  P  T  D  X
Z  R  M  D  R  E  Z  W  B  G
B  L  V  L  R  S  N  O  Z  K
N  M  R  C  A  C  E  F  L  B
P  H  E  W  C  S  V  T  K  C
```

KAYA   RIVER   MAGPIE
NEZ PERCE   VALLEY   RAIDERS
SALMON   HORSE

Answers in the back of the book.

ON THE MAP

When Kaya escapes from the enemy tribe, she uses the stars
and familiar landmarks to find her way home. Use the space
below to draw a map of your neighborhood. Include landmarks
that a friend could use to find a path to your home.

MEET FELICITY

NAME: Felicity Merriman

NICKNAME: Lissie

HOME: Williamsburg, Virginia

HAIR: Red

EYES: Green

PERSONALITY: Felicity is fiercely loyal, independent, and spirited

YEAR: 1774

Felicity loves riding horses far more than quiet, ladylike activities such as stitchery.

Felicity and her siblings visit their grandfather at his plantation.

Felicity is supposed to politely serve tea. Instead, she and Annabelle argue about politics!

FELICITY'S COLONIAL WORD SEARCH

Find and circle the words listed below by searching up, down, forward, backward, and diagonally.

P L F R X O Y A W L
T C Q C Z L I B I P
S O K N R N R X L K
B L O Z I E O A L U
T O E G E W N I I I
K N R C N T O J A E
L I H C A K L M M T
V E P T J Q C D S A
S S I N S H S S B L
Y O R K T O W N U O
N R A T I U G T R C
R C B M H D N O G O
T A O C I T T E P H
F K B F S U O E Q C

WILLIAMSBURG   COLONIES   PETTICOAT
VIRGINIA   PLANTATION   GUITAR
YORKTOWN   BREECHES   CHOCOLATE

Answers in the back of the book.

NOT IN THIS PICTURE

This picture might look like the same image of Felicity's tea with friends, but it's not. Several items are not in the picture. Can you pick out the items that are missing in the scene?

Go back and take a look at the picture on page 11. Stare at it for five seconds to commit it to memory. Then come back to this page to test your memory.

Answers in the back of the book.

MEET JOSEFINA

NAME: María Josefina Montoya

HOME: New Mexico

HAIR: Dark Brown

EYES: Brown

DREAMS OF: Becoming a *curandera*, or healer

YEAR: 1824

Josefina and her sisters are thrilled to meet
their aunt, Tía Dolores, for the first time.

Josefina loves her mother's handmade doll, Niña. Her sister Clara
sewed a new dress for Niña and gave her to Josefina for Christmas.

Papá plays his violin for the family for the first time since Mamá passed away.

MEMORY BOOK

Josefina's Tia Dolores made a memory book and filled it with her favorite memories from when she was a child. Fill in the blanks below to make your own memory journal.

Name:

Best friend:

Age:

Best class in school:

Nickname:

Use three words to describe yourself:

Favorite book:

What do you want to be when you grow up?

Favorite movie:

Do you have a pet? If so, what's their name?

Favorite holiday:

What has been your best birthday and why?

Favorite food:

Favorite thing to do on a sunny day:

Favorite American Girl:

Favorite thing to do on a rainy day:

JOSEFINA'S WORLD

Place the words in the crossword puzzle below
that match the information about Josefina.

ACROSS

1. Last name

3. Musical instrument her father plays

6. Eye color

7. Her mother's doll

8. Hair color

DOWN

2. First name

4. Sister

5. Home

MEET KIRSTEN

NAME: Kirsten Larson

HOME: Minnesota

HAIR: Blonde

EYES: Light Blue

PERSONALITY: Brave and steadfast

YEAR: 1854

Kirsten's teacher, Miss Winston, shows her a ship in a bottle that looks
just like the ship Kirsten's family sailed on from Sweden to America.

Kirsten, her little brother, Peter, and Peter's dog, Caro, find a baby bear cub.
When the mama bear emerges from the forest, Kirsten, Peter, and Caro flee to safety.

Kirsten goes trapping in the forest with her
brother Lars and his friend John Stewart.

AT HOME WITH KIRSTEN

Kirsten's family were pioneers, and they lived in a log cabin.
What kind of house would you like to live in? Draw it here.

DRAW KIRSTEN

Using the grid as a guide, draw Kirsten below.

MEET ADDY

NAME: Aduke Walker

NICKNAME: Addy

HOME: Philadelphia, Pennsylvania

HAIR: Dark Brown

EYES: Brown

DREAMS OF: Reuniting with her family in freedom

YEAR: 1864

Addy and Momma escape slavery disguised as a boy and a man. After many dangers, they arrive at Miss Caroline's, their first stop on the Underground Railroad.

Addy goes to school for the first time in Philadelphia, where she learns
how to read and write. She then teaches Momma her lessons after school.

Poppa reunites with the family in Philadelphia. They plant a
garden to raise funds for a trip to find the rest of Addy's family.

SPELLING MATCH

Addy won the spelling match in her class, which included the following words. Can you complete the words from her spelling match by filling in the missing letters from the jumble of letters at the top? (Cross out each letter when you use it to remove it from the jumble.)

T R G B C C O T S R
I G L W T R U C S M R
G B U S M N

1. CA __ __ I A __ E
(A mode of transportation)

2. __ U __ T O __
(Something sewn on clothes)

3. __ O __ O R R __ __
(The next day)

4. AC __ O __ N __
(A record of money spent and received)

5. __ R __ D __ E
(A structure spanning a waterway or road)

6. S __ I __ __ O __ S
(A tool to cut paper or cloth)

7. P __ I N __ I P __ E
(A moral guide)

NOT IN THIS PICTURE

This picture might look like the same image of Addy in her classroom, but it's not. Several items are missing. Can you pick out the items that are missing in the scene?

Go back and take a look at the picture on page 28. Stare at it for five seconds to commit it to memory. Then come back to this page to test your memory.

Answers in the back of the book.

MEET SAMANTHA

NAME: Samantha Parkington

NICKNAME: Sam

HOME: Mount Bedford, New York

HAIR: Dark Brown   EYES: Brown

DREAMS OF: Having a family of her own

YEAR: 1904

Samantha falls out of an oak tree in Grandmary's backyard
when her neighbor Eddie Ryland surprises her.

Samantha's friend Nellie had never gone to school before,
so Samantha tutors her in reading and writing after school.

After seeing children working in factories and the daily dangers they face,
Samantha gives a speech about child labor at her school's speaking contest.

DRAW SAMANTHA

Using the grid as a guide, draw Samantha below.

SAMANTHA'S WORLD

Place the words in the crossword puzzle below
that match the information about Samantha.

ACROSS

1. Last name

5. A subject she taught Nellie

7. Home

DOWN

2. Name she calls her grandmother

3. Neighbor

4. Friend she tutors

6. Eye color

8. Type of tree

MEET REBECCA

NAME: Rebecca Rubin

NICKNAME: Beckie

HOME: Lower East Side of New York City

HAIR: Brown

DREAMS OF: Being an actress

YEAR: 1914

EYES: Hazel

At Sabbath dinner, Rebecca pantomimes a story that
her cousin Max—a real actor!—tells by candlelight.

Rebecca visits a movie set and meets the beautiful star, Lily Armstrong.
And her dream comes true when she gets a surprise role in the movie.

After seeing the horrible conditions at the factory where her uncle and cousin work, Rebecca joins a protest and even makes a speech at a Labor Day picnic.

REBECCA'S WORLD WORD SEARCH

Find and circle the words listed below by searching up,
down, forward, backward, and diagonally.

ACTOR	FACTORY	PICNIC
CANDLE	HANUKKAH	SABBATH
DINNER	MOVIE	TEACHER

Answers in the back of the book.

DOG GONE

Maryellen's beloved dachshund, Scooter, has gone missing. Maryellen and her sister must look for him in the forest. Follow the path below to get him from lost to found.

LOST

FOUND

MEET MELODY

NAME: Melody Ellison

NICKNAME: Dee-Dee

HOME: Detroit, Michigan

HAIR: Dark Brown

EYES: Brown

DREAMS OF: A world in which everyone is treated equally

YEAR: 1964

Melody is thrilled when her brother, Dwayne, asks her to
sing backup as he records his first single at a music studio.

When Melody's older sister Yvonne isn't allowed to apply for a job at
the bank because she is black, Melody protests by closing her account.

Melody and her family listen to Martin Luther King Jr. speak at the Walk to Freedom civil rights march. Melody is inspired by his speech to sing her favorite song at the Youth Day concert.

A SONG IN YOUR HEART

Melody loves to sing and listen to her brother play music.
What are some of your favorite songs? Answer the
questions below. Then write your own song!

What song do you like to
listen to when you're sad?

_____

What is your favorite song that
came out before you were born?

_____

What is your favorite
song to dance to?

_____

What is your all-time
favorite song?

_____

If you could write a song, what
would you want to sing about?
Use the space below to start a song of your own . . .

_____

_____

_____

_____

_____

_____

_____

_____

_____

_____

NOT IN THIS PICTURE

This picture might look like the same image of Melody's recording session with her brother, but it's not. Several items are missing. Can you pick out the items that are missing in the scene?

Go back and take a look at the picture on page 69. Stare at it for five seconds to commit it to memory. Then come back to this page to test your memory.

Answers in the back of the book.

MEET JULIE

NAME: Julie Albright

NICKNAMES: Alley Oop, Jules, and Cool Hands Albright

HOME: San Francisco, California

HAIR: Blonde   EYES: Brown

PERSONALITY: Creative, upbeat, and outspoken

YEAR: 1974

Julie and her best friend, Ivy, celebrate Chinese New Year in San Francisco.

Julie loves to play basketball, but she can't join the all-boys team. Julie learns that the Title IX law grants equal rights for girls to play sports in public schools, and she petitions for the right to join the team.

Julie volunteers at a wildlife shelter and organizes a class campaign on
Earth Day to help reintroduce a family of bald eagles to the wild.

FEED THE BIRDS?

Julie uses a puppet to help feed a baby bird that was separated from its mama. Follow the paths below to figure out which one will get the food in the puppet's beak to the baby bird.

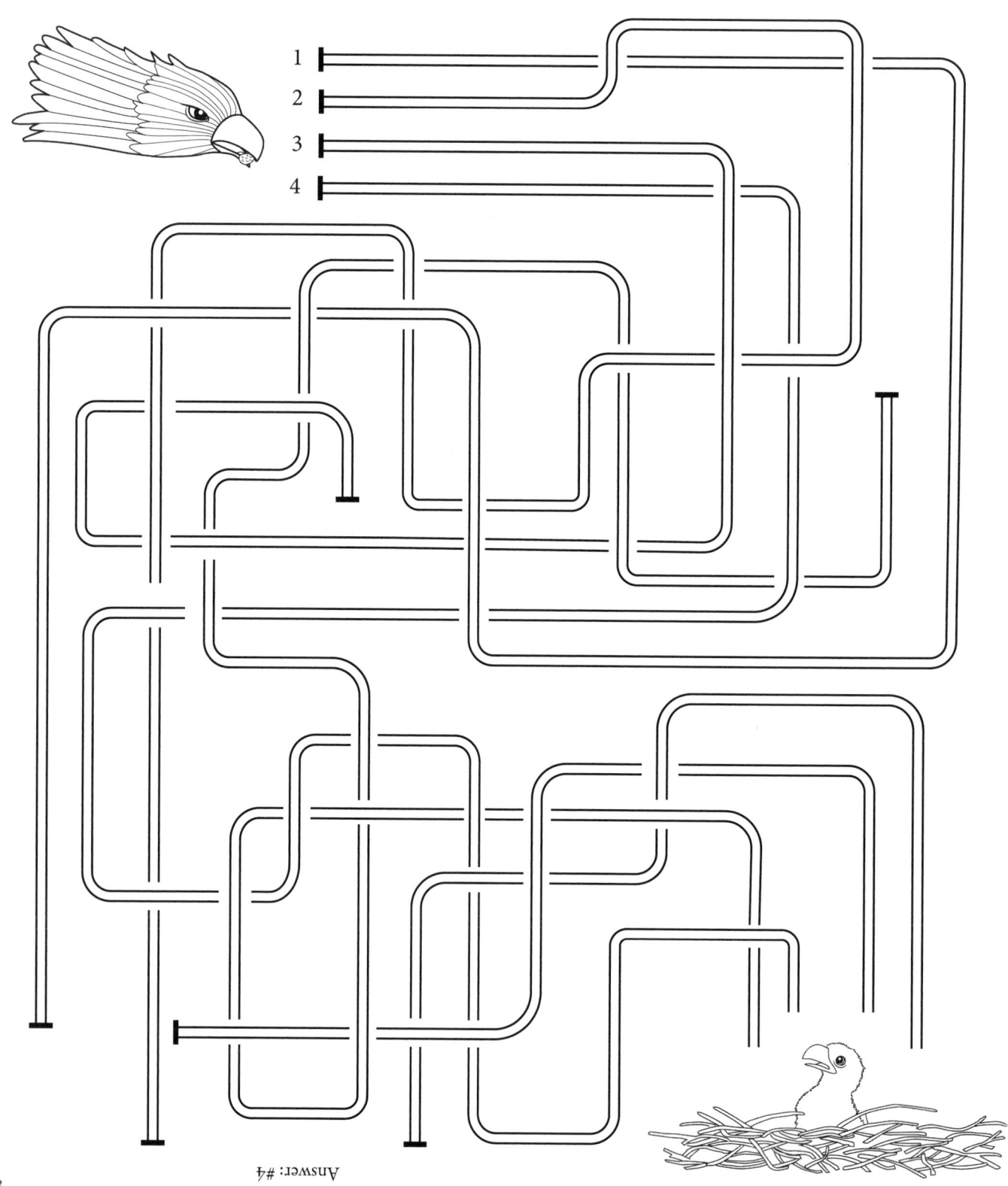

Answer: #4

DECORATING WITH JULIE

Julie is very creative and decorated her room with her mom's help. If you could redecorate your room, how would you change it? Draw it below.

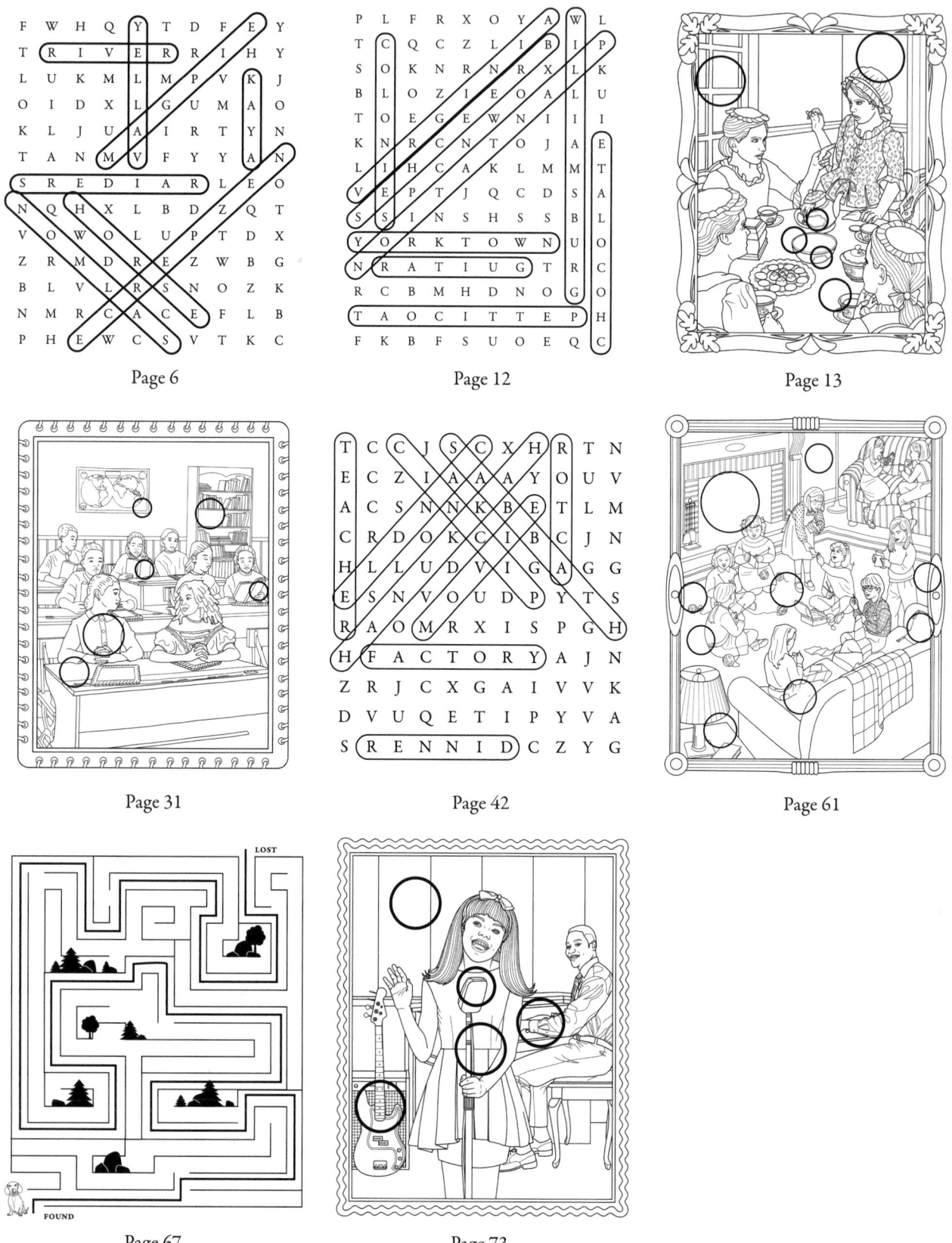

Page 6

Page 12

Page 13

Page 31

Page 42

Page 61

Page 67

Page 73